Joanne

Every new beginning comes from some other beginnings end!

Hunter Dan

Joanne & 13.11

Every new beginning comes
from some other beginning's
end!

Martin Dan

Inspirations and Emotions

Seven Layers to the Truth

Hunter Dan

iUniverse

Inspirations and Emotions
Seven Layers to the Truth

Copyright © 2015 Hunter Dan.

All rights reserved. No part of this book may be used or reproduced by any means, graphic, electronic, or mechanical, including photocopying, recording, taping or by any information storage retrieval system without the written permission of the publisher except in the case of brief quotations embodied in critical articles and reviews.

iUniverse books may be ordered through booksellers or by contacting:

iUniverse
1663 Liberty Drive
Bloomington, IN 47403
www.iuniverse.com
1-800-Authors (1-800-288-4677)

Because of the dynamic nature of the Internet, any web addresses or links contained in this book may have changed since publication and may no longer be valid. The views expressed in this work are solely those of the author and do not necessarily reflect the views of the publisher, and the publisher hereby disclaims any responsibility for them.

Any people depicted in stock imagery provided by Thinkstock are models, and such images are being used for illustrative purposes only. Certain stock imagery © Thinkstock.

ISBN: 978-1-4917-6433-6 (sc)
ISBN: 978-1-4917-6434-3 (e)

Print information available on the last page.

iUniverse rev. date: 06/05/2015

About the Author

My name is Daniel J. Hamel. I was born June 13th 1964. My birth mothers name was Shirley Ann Fisher. My birth father, I have no information on who he was. My name at birth was Timothy John Chandler. At age 6 months I along with my year and a half old sister Gwen were taken away from our mother by the state of Vt. and put up for adoption. Our 3 year old brother Fred was allowed to stay. She was determined to be unfit to raise 3 children alone as an alcoholic.

Gwen and I were adopted separately by two different families. I was adopted by Ronald and Madelyne Hamel of Windsor Vt. I was the youngest of 5 children and graduated in 1982 from Windsor High School. I have one son named Joseph Timothy from my first marriage. He was born November 1st 1988. He has blessed me with my only grandchild Jack Joseph and very influential aspect to my sobriety.

I have battled the disease myself over the years. In the fall of 2011 I started writing poetry. Several were written before I got sober while I was married to my second wife. As that marriage was failing I continued to write. When we separated in January 2014 we still loved each other but I wasn't the man she married. A month later on February 23rd she took me to rehab which saved my life. I continued to write in rehab and in sobriety afterward as Jennifer and I worked on our marriage. In October of 2014 I made a decision I didn't want her son to be a part of my life. We were divorced in December.

A Hunters Prayer

By Hunter Dan

Every day is Sunday when I sit upon my perch, that's because I believe the woods are my church. I believe in him and I worship thee. I'm closer to him when I'm sitting in a tree. The critters do their thing on the ground down below. I hear the caw from a distant crow. Every bird, every squirrel that I see throughout the day, reminds me, don't get busted by a blue jay. I sit there still as I would in a pew, waiting patiently for the chosen few. It's not just a kill or the meat that I crave, it's being one with nature and the memories that I save.

As I watch all the animals that happen to come by, I'm closer to him because I say whether they live or die. I do not harvest what I wouldn't eat. All animals are a blessing that pass beneath my feet. Most of them taken don't feel any pain, their time has come to become a link in the food chain. Any person that doesn't understand what we do can go to church on Sunday and sit in a pew. I'd never put down or judge what they do, because I'm up in my stand

worshiping the view.

We pay our dues and endure the cold. I'll climb up a tree and hunt till I'm too old. Even then I'm not sure I will stop, as my ashes can be spread in my favorite spot. To the posted landowner, yes it's considered a sport, I was taught to share, life is too short. We ask for permission, we respect the land because in all actuality you're only leasing it from the man. He created it all for all to enjoy. It was his vision from the time he was a boy. Every day is Sunday when HE sits on his perch. That's because he believes

the woods are his church.

Inspirations and Emotions | 1

I am a Tree

By Hunter Dan

It's hard to believe, I started as a seed. Although it's taken many years, inch by inch I've grown bigger than my peers. I enjoy the moon, I love the sun. In the spring when I sprout buds I know the winter is done.

This is the time birds like the best, my leaves as they grow disguise their nests. As the months get warmer and the summer gets hotter, I crave the rain because I need the water. A little is ok, but I don't mind longer, my roots get more it makes then stronger.

As summer goes by, warm days start to fade, I'm a great place for a picnic because I will always provide shade. Then comes autumn, I hear the call. My leaves turn brown and gold, soon they will fall.

Now the nest can be seen and the grass below is no longer green. The nights get cool, the days getting so, it gets really cold when the wind starts to blow. When it stops you can hear every sound, reality sets in when snow hits the ground. The squirrels store their nuts in my many hiding places, so when snow is on the ground they can still fill their faces.

Winter is here, I'll survive, I know I can. It's Mother Nature's cycle starting all over again. I enjoy every season, I'm here for a reason. I'm just being me but I'm not just a tree!

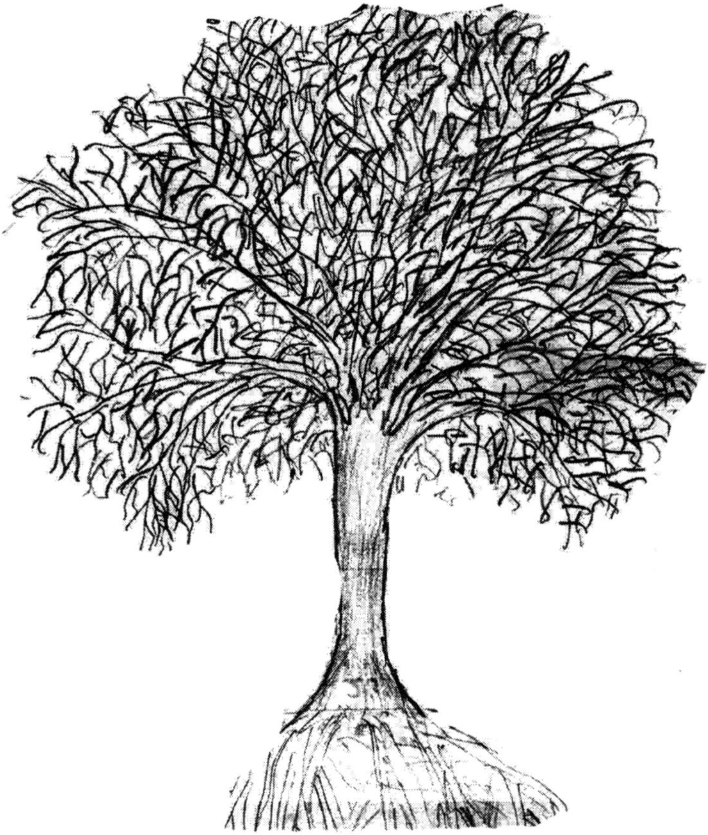

SPIRIT OF THE WOODS

By Hunter Dan

I went in the woods to go for a walk. I went alone and didn't have to talk. As I walked down a trail I felt alone, but thats far from the truth, I should have known. I'm not the only living thing in this place, every creature, tree and bush is alive that I face. There's a dead tree whose trunk has failed. It fell to the ground and redirected the trail. I walk to be silent to keep the woods as they are. I want to keep going I just don't know how far. Every tree that I pass, if they could talk, I bet they would say, "I wish I could walk". Unfortunately they are stuck to their roots, I'm sure if they could they would trade them for boots.

There goes a red squirrel, he just grabbed a pine cone. He's probably taking it back to his home. I'm not sure what he has for a plan, I don't know how he can use it, if he even can. In hunters terminology I just jumped a deer. I didn't see what it was because the cold made my eyes tear. There is a little snow on the ground, hunting season is done. Nobody else in the woods I'm the only one. Not enough snow to snowmobile or for a cross country skier, I'm just walking down the trail not causing any fear. So I think, there's a fischer cat at the brook taking a drink. They are nasty creatures and they don't play fair. They are deadly to family pets and they just don't care.

I see plenty of birds flying all around, some up in trees, some on the ground. They try to get every morsal they can, look, theres a partridge strutting with a full fan. I would like to keep going but I may have gone too far. I should turn around and head back to my car. Now the sun is in my eyes, I'm going to have to squint, I'll keep my eyes on the ground and follow my foot prints. As I head back I just jumped a buck. I'll see him next saeson if I have a little luck. I didn't get a good look at his horns, he was digging in the snow to get some acorns.

As I work my way back, I take it all in. When I got back to my car I couldn't help but grin. The life, peace and quiet that I just endured, to anyone in the city it would be the cure. We have it to share if they choose to come. If they stay in the city it's really kind of dumb. When you think about it, it doesn't cost a thing, to walk through the woods and hear the birds sing. To those who do, they know who has the goods. For me, I love the spirit of the woods.

SPEAK THE LANGUAGE

By Hunter Dan

In the spring I love to go, It falls before summer, fully dressed in camo. It's turkey season on the first of May. Through all of April I can't wait for the day. It breaks up the year and it's a totally different season, hunting the wild turkey for a totally different reason. Turkeys don't have the willingness as deer to stand face to face and confront their fear. I locate them at dusk by hooting like an owl. They will even answer to a coyote howl. I have them located when they fly up on the roost. When the alarm sounds at 3:30 I jump out of bed with a boost. I drive to the spot and I'm wide awake. I get myself set up and wait for the day to break. They gobble like crazy up in the tree. When they fly down I think they are coming to me.

I hope they don't already have a hen roosted up above, so when I call they instantly fall in love. The gobbles get closer as my heart starts to pound. My decoys are setup out in front of me on the ground. Twenty five yards out in front of my sight, when he sees the jake I hope he's ready to fight. If it's a longbeard he is sure to try to steal the hen away from the jake that isn't real.

The gobbles are close as I rest the gun on my knee. I finally see him coming around a tree. He spots the decoys and quickens his pace. Here comes another, it's turned into a race. They go right for the jake to beat him up, then they will court the hen by strutting their stuff. They kick and peck the jake looking at him strange, not realizing that I have them in range. They focus on the hen fanned out looking to please, I steady on ones head and get ready to squeeze. I tagged him and loaded him, and smile as I turn the key, knowing how hard it is to outwit a turkey. I encouraged him to exploit his rage, He is in the truck because I speak the language.

Dog is God Spelled Backwards

By Hunter Dan

Dog is God when you turn it around.
One is worshiped in heaven, the other on the ground.
One you can see, the other you can't.
One speaks silently, the other just pants.
They both unconditionally love and they do not judge.
You can cross either one and they won't hold a grudge.
One can always see you, the other may just stare.
Be kind to both and they will always be there.
God is his name, it will never change.
A dog you can call anything no matter how strange.
One watches over you, the other will follow you.
There's no greater loyalty than what you will receive from these two.
They are both very different, yet very much the same.
One can punish you, the other takes the blame.
God you can't see, you know he's always there.
A dog will take a nap next to you while you're sitting in the chair.
A dog you can teach tricks. They can do so many things.
God teaches you when you pass how to use your wings.

THINKING OF YOU

By Hunter Dan

It's amazing how fast a life can come to an end, a father, mother, brother, sister, child or a friend. It's a journey in time that has come to a seize, whether you crash, get shot, burn or you freeze. There are so many ways it can come to a halt and it doesn't even have to be your own fault.

Twenty six lives woke up one morning, not knowing it was the last as it came with no warning. Twenty were innocent children living six years give or take. They filled churches and funeral homes with people at their wake. Six passed as heroes being adults, saving the survivors like they locked them in vaults.

It wasn't fair to anyone in that school, how one messed up young man could be so cruel. The first responders and parents not believing what they had seen, prayed that it was all a bad dream. But it was not, and a nation shared a tear. Nobody should ever have to live with such fear. It was just a small school on this side of the water. It goes to show how precious a child's life is whether it's a son or a daughter. Don't ever miss a chance to give your child a kiss, as it could end in an instant in a tragedy like this.

I could go on and on and probably write a book, when all I want to do is reach out to Sandy Hook. We know every day is going to be tough, and whatever we do will never be enough. Just know we will do all that we can do, but most of all take comfort in knowing we are thinking of you.

WE CAME BACK AS CARDINALS

By Hunter Dan

It was only the beginning when you laid us to rest, we came back as cardinals and our story is the best. Now when we speak our voices just sing. We are the free'est of birds since God gave us wings. It's true what they say when they say life never ends, we can fly all around and visit our friends. We know you've all seen us we just drop on by. We only want to see you, there's no other reason why. It's not that we are worried because we don't have a care. We are just two red birds that want to be there.

We'll stay a while if we see a need, we'll stay for dinner if you put out some seed. Jen often feeds us but hasn't for a while, we know that she's busy so we fly off with a smile. We fly down the river it's a beautiful flight, we can do it in an hour if the wind is just right. Most of the time we are in no hurry. When you're free as a bird you don't have a worry. We stop in Ascutney at Andy and Carlenes. Her feeders are full the most I've ever seen. We visit for a while and head over to the granite state. It's a short flight to Pine Hill to see Craig and Kate. Many of their neighbors fill their feeders every day, it's good to see them, it's like an all day buffet. As the sun goes down and the day comes to an end, we have a favorite pine tree where we spend the night with a friend. When day breaks and we've rested our souls, we take off to Franklin to Matt and Nicoles.

That's a long flight, it's an all day affair, it's pretty much dark by the time we get there. We know what we are in for because we show up with no warning, so we nest in their pine tree and see them in the morning. The next leg of our journey takes pretty long, we leave Matt and Nicole singing a song. We enjoy it for sure, it does us no harm. We are headed to Vershire to see Kevin on the farm.

He has some large birds that can't even fly, God gave them wings and they don't even try. To complete the final leg of our plan, it's off to Northfield where it all began. As many miles as we have flown, this is where we call our home. The trip around the family circle makes us happy, keep an eye out the window for Nanny and Pappy.

A DAMN YANKEE

By Hunter Dan

He's just another one of those old timers who is stricken with the disease known as Alzheimers. He was the smartest man I ever knew, now he sits in a chair and doesn't have a clue. For the last few years you would see him get tense, now he can't even finish a sentence.

I think he knows who we are which makes it rough. Dot's world has turned upside down and has become tough. She has done extremely well and works hard every day. Because he won't eat he will wither away. He needs help with simple chores, and he can't even walk outdoors. Which is a blessing unknown to itself, because he would leave not knowing where he was going. It's not fair to her, it's not what she signed up for, she shouldn't have to do it anymore. They were great for each other having been through much of the same, but now he doesn't even know her name. It's hard to see his life go in this direction, but seeing my grandfather go through it there is definitely a connection.

We as his children have to do what's best, he needs special care until we lay him to rest. To Dot we owe you a big thank you, there's nothing more we expect from you. He has made it to the top of his golden years. Risking injury to you is what we fear. His favorite team is from the Bronx, I don't know how that could be, but he will go down in history as a damn Yankee!

ORPHAN ANN AND HER BROTHER DAN

By Hunter Dan

Five decades ago a sister and her brother were taken away from their mother. She was a year and a half, he was six months. For forty years they didn't see each other once. Adopted away each to a different family, probably again each other would never see. They both did well in their new role. Knowing their past not each other would take a toll. Both families were honest, they loved them and let them know, it was for the best their mother had to let them go.

As the years went by, they grew and became adults. Dan started digging and had some results. Knowing where he was born he continued to dig. He found information that turned out big. The state would only give non identifying information, what he discovered gave him a sensation. His mother's name he was able to find, and where she worked in that town there were only two of that kind. The first didn't pan out so he went to the other. He found a woman who was willing to talk about his mother. With regret he found out almost three months to the day, his mother had developed pneumonia and had passed away. Saddened as he was he found he had a brother, not only one but there was another. Not only that there were two sisters too. He had discovered a family he never knew. The kind woman gave their names and said, "they all live in town." He found a phone number and his birth family was found.

They planned a reunion and it was all you would think, except orphan Ann was the missing link. As years went by Dan tried to find Ann. He was determined to complete the family trying as hard as he can. Always running into a dead end, one day he received a message his long lost sister would send. It was from an employee of the state, Ann had found him and the news was great. The missing link had been found, and a meeting was set. It was a day in their lives they will never forget. Meeting for dinner half way in between was a happy ending to a forty year dream. Swapping stories of growing up with the families they had, it was all very happy only one story sad. The parents who had adopted her, tried to get him, but the state would deter. They couldn't go together, they weren't sure why. The state wouldn't allow it even though they did try.

Funny thing is when he was adopted and given his new start, the families only lived fifteen miles apart. Now they have all been reunited and know each other happily, they all have learned about their family tree. Not certain of the outcome but thinking they can, reunited forever are orphan Ann and her brother Dan.

HAPPY MOTHERS DAY

For sixteen years this has been your home. I can't imagine it's been that long, I never would have known. It doesn't seem that long ago, you moved on and left us to grow. Time goes by so very fast. Another year gone they just don't last. Mother's Day seemed a good time to come. To wait sixteen years I feel ashamed and dumb. It's hard to visit with such small talk. There's plenty of parking and it's such a short walk. I brought a chair to sit and think. When I get thirsty I have water to drink. I would offer some but you would just say no. Take what you don't drink with you when you go.

Last August on the 24th day, dad made reservations now he's here to stay. I'm sure you don't mind his company. You probably wondered where the hell he could be. For fifteen years he lived his life, without you but with a new wife. She was great to him and you should be glad. The Christian in you couldn't possibly be mad. It's very peaceful sitting in your yard. Gathering my thoughts doesn't seem hard. I'm writing as they come to me. I look at your neighbors looking back at me. As I read I see their face, so many friends have moved into this place.

The breeze feels good, the sun is hot. You moved in to a very peaceful spot. The trees all around are starting to bloom. This place almost full there's not much more room. The birds chirp as the traffic flows by, you probably would sit up and ask yourself why. Or maybe not as you really can't do, I'm here visiting out of respect for you.

At 22 months I didn't have a home, so you took me back to your own. You gave me a life, because you were willing to add number five. I'm sure many times you second guessed that, when I didn't come home and you said, "where the heck is he at?" By number five I figured you were tired of getting mad, but you both let me know when I had been bad. Now I know what you meant when your fist gave a wave, and you shouted the words, "I'll swear on my grave". Now here we are I am listening to you. I'm waiting for you to tell me what to do.

I'm almost 50 years old and I've run my last course, I'm tired and going through my second divorce. I learned from you to work hard every day. And you are never too old to go out and play. So as I write the answers come to me, don't dictate your life, just let it be. Now that I've been here I hope I can come again. I promise I will,
I'm just not sure when.

Maybe next month when dad has his day, we'll leave it at that and continue to pray. I believe in God, you taught me that. I'm in the process now of where I'll find him at. I'm sorry it took me so long to say, "Happy Mother's Day," at your grave. It's goodbye for now, I will see you again. Happy Mother's Day,

Love your son and your friend!

THE LIFE AND TIMES OF JAKE HENNE

By Hunter Dan

It happened in 1963 the nation lost John F. Kennedy. But that same year was a surprise to me, the world gained John, Jackie, Jake Henne. In 1967 living on Ascutney St. two young boys living next to each other finally did meet. Too young to know what life had in store, in 2013 we still want more.

When they moved away the Hennes disappeared. Later in life Chris Curtis appeared. In between I had many a friend, we had a tight neighborhood and alot of time we would spend. We played sports and malty and had lots of fun. But when they moved away I thought a friendship was done. Straight out of Jackass they thought this was cool. Flying down Martinsville Rd. they would go. Starting to swerve on the bank with a thump, quickley learned a stump you can't jump. They rolled over and over, every corner of the car had bends. When I found out, I almost lost my two friends.

After high school we all did our thing. Chris in the Navy, John, Jackie, Jake tried his hand at everything. We worked at Sids, brother Bill as our boss. There may have been nights of some memory loss. Those were the days, Luigi, McCarthy, Buddy and the crew. Then in the back I remember was Nelson too. In our 20's when I had a son, Jake lived life like I should have done. He moved to Lake George and lived in a camper by himself. Then he moved to Nashville to discover his wealth. In Nashville he lived, Lake George sat by a fire, those two moves you can't help but admire.

He then bought a house and began to settle down. Not knowing his future or what was in store, he built a butcher shop to cut deer and more. He soon graduated to cutting up steer, he quickley grew and the business had to move. Now it's so big he is in his groove.

He has a remarkable, talented, very smart daughter who if she wanted could walk on water. He is smart and has always followed his dream, that is why he is married to the beautiful Koreen.

BEING THERE WAS THE BEST

By Hunter Dan

It was a goal that put him to the test as DJ said, "being there was the best." The stands full of fans chanting his name, you know he wanted to be on his game. It was low scoring from the start. David knew he had to play his part. He took some shots that just didn't fall, and when he had to he passed the ball. I was proud to be there and see it play out. At the end when he got it I could barely shout.

The first half ended, he was off the pace. He needed 22 points to raise the roof off that place. With the clock winding down stuck at 19, he dribbled to the corner and got the shot off clean. 11 seconds to go the ball swished through the hoop, he ran to his family and they hugged as a group. His primary goal was to win the game, his secondary goal was to hoist his name. He is an awesome kid who never said forget, he kept his head up until the ball fell through the net.

He got to 1000 points and the pressure is done. He can finish the season and play because it is fun. I write my poems and sign them Hunter Dan, David knows who I am, I'm a friend and a fan.

A KICK OF HOPE

By Hunter Dan

There is a young man who has a disability, his mind may be slowed but his body has the ability. His name is Anthony, last name Starego. Invite him to a Rutgers game and he is sure to go. If Rutgers searched for their biggest fan, they wouldn't have to look beyond this young man. Anthony went to his dad one day after a Rutgers game and said," I want to play".

His dad in shock and with disbelief, said to himself the school won't believe. Anthony has a smile that warms your heart. His story will rip your tear ducts apart. Playing a sport you have to be tough. As a journalist you can't make up this stuff. The pride and happiness his parents displayed, there is no doubt they are glad he played. It was easy to understand their fear. His story on ESPN made you shed a tear.

Nothing can make you understand quicker than to watch Brick High School's field goal kicker. He nailed the kick that won the game. Their rival team will remember his name. As with kickers you often have to cope. His dad said it best, it was a kick of hope.

JACK AND ROBERT

By Hunter Dan

I got bit by Jack Frost and turned into Robert Frost. I am a truck driver whose two cents come at no cost. When you drive for a living, you have time to invent ways of giving. Here is my donation in life. Be a good dad to your kids, and cherish your wife. They grow up fast, help with home work, attend their games, before you know, it's in the past. Tuck them in, read them a story as much as you can. Leave them smiling and they will be your biggest fan.

Teach them early to be kind. Discipline will pay off, it's what you will find. Provide them with the best you can. They will look up to you like you are the man. It's a simple formula any man can do, it's just some are different because they choose to. Look back at how you were raised, because it's never too late to offer them praise. Thank them for the memories you saved, even if you thank them at their grave. I started out by writing one poem, here I am four years later, still going and going. I wait for a title that touches me, I grab a pencil and let it be free.

Some times I just sit and think, the pencil writes better if I've had a drink. It is still winter and it's very cold. I'm glad Jack bit me before I'm too old. Writng poems is a pretty neat job, I'm glad Jack bit me and turned me into Rob.

My Best Friend

By Hunter Dan

A simple text is what I send. To remind you, you are my best friend. I don't need to remind me, I know in my heart you will always be. I knew it when we said "I Do". I'm so happy that God introduced me to you. It felt so right from the very first date, we fell in love and it felt like fate. Even though we don't always see eye to eye, I want the world to know I am your guy. When we are together I don't want it to end. I can't get enough of my best friend.

I see you in a different light, now when I'm wrong I want to make it right. Your smile and your innocence makes me feel my love for you is truly for real. Thinking back my blessings are what I should be counting, after all when I proposed I dragged you up a mountain. To get you to the top I encouraged and teased, when I showed you the ring you were more than pleased. You were tired and exhausted but that was replaced by the kiss that you gave me and the look on your face. At the top of the road to nowhere, where it finally does end, I gave my heart to

my best friend.

That place has the most amazing view. But I just couldn't take my eyes off from you. It was a nice hike but probably not fair, the walk down was easy because you were walking on air. I cherish that spot, it means so much to me. It's where the sky meets the mountains for as far as you can see. To climb up there now it's all I can do, I am so happy I was able to share it with you. It's one of those spots that I've always said, "When I've passed I want a few ashes spread". I know it's a long time from now and who really knows when, but I know I can count on

my best friend.

From now on please hear what I've said. I believe for me and you, our best years are ahead. With so much to fix and wrinkles to smooth, our future together will greatly improve. The days of tears and valleys of sorrow will be replaced with love and sunshine tomorrow. One day at a time each with no expectation, it will develop and flourish as one of God's own creations. I hope you are willing to go along for the ride. Hold my hand on this journey standing by my side. It's a journey in time with no room for a bend. I feel confident with you as

my best friend.

If just talking and we share a laugh, holding you while we take a bath. Cuddling while we watch TV, looking at you while you look at me. Smiling as you walk out the door, saddened you leave because I just want more. Hunter Dan and Jennifer Lynn some day will be together again. I know it's true, and I know we can because there is no doubt you are

my best friend.

Gin before Jen

By Hunter Dan

On April 18th 2009, from that day forward I thought we would be fine. On that day I married my best friend. Barely into 2014 is it really the end? I took Jen to have and to hold, for better or for worse until we grow old. We even agreed on sickness and in health. Through several operations that jeopardized our wealth.

No matter what the circumstances would bring she never worried about a thing. We stood together, her by my side, then one day she found the secret that I hide. Caught red handed I take the blame. It's a secret we kept as we both were ashamed. I drank gin and kept it from all. It was my secret weapon that made me 10 feet tall. As time went by it only got worse. It went from a bad habit to our relationship curse. I would drink before I got home. I knew she could tell by the sound of her tone.

Over a period of the 3rd and 4th year, my habit worsened and included beer. I blamed it on an unhappy job. I turned to gin not Jen and became a slob. I needed a change. I couldn't do that job anymore. My body was tired so I changed at the risk of being poor. Jen helped me get a job hauling gas. Working nights we both hoped this drinking thing would pass. We didn't see each other much at all. If we talked it was mostly with a phone call. The marriage suffered, our friendship started to lack. Regardless of all this she still had my back.

Over these years I'd sip the gin straight with total disregard of my mate. It came to be so important to me. I lost track of who I was supposed to be. So many hiding spots in the garage, I find a reason to go out and recharge. She caught onto this and searched for whatever it was in, when she found it she would dump the gin. I would throw the empty in the trash and find the money to buy another one to stash. Just a few sips I would take them quick, not realizing just how much I was sick. It was Jen I should have invested in, to my loving wife I kept committing this sin.

October 2011 again thinking of I, helping an injured man I got a DUI. I convinced myself and the judge it was isolated. When in all actuality it was really outdated. Drinking and driving didn't scare me. Looking back at it now how lucky would I be. I would drink and drive and not really care, I was convinced my license and wife were still going to be there. While I prioritized the gin and beer, Jen hung on for another year. Even though I could see us fade, when the bottle emptied another purchase was made.

The bottle was clear, to the other side you could see. What wasn't clear was what it was doing to me. For the longest time I medicated myself, not bothered by what it was doing to my health. Hunting season 2011 one morning in my truck I wrote as I sit, a secretive poem titled, I Urned it. I knew back then if I didn't quit I would die. But for two more years I continued to lie. At night as the best thing that ever happened to me went to sleep, I would sneak out to the garage for the poison that I keep. It was what I needed I had convinced my head. But what I really needed was asleep in our bed.

Now in March 2014 a month after Jen took me to get clean. She promised that she would wait for me. As scared as I was I needed to become alcohol free. Even though we separated in January, picturing the future was more than scary. I know being sober is priority number one in my life. I can't help but think what I have done to my wife. My lowest of low has taken me to zero. What she has done for me makes her my hero.

She stood by me though I continued to drink. How much can a wife put up with is unimaginable to think. Now that I'm sober our future up in the air. It's comforting to know that she can even still care. It's difficult because I love her more than she will ever know, what's even harder is letting go. That is the position that I find myself in. All because I didn't put Jen before Gin. Now I don't drink and I owe that to my wife. I will love her no matter what happens for the rest of my life. If we do get back together only God knows when. We would still be together if I hadn't put Gin before Jen.

HER SMILE

By Hunter Dan

When I opened my eyes in the morning, I saw her smile. When I kissed her good morning, I saw her smile. When I brought her coffee in the morning as she got ready for work, I saw her smile. When I told her how pretty she looked, I saw her smile. When I kissed her good bye and said," I love you", I saw her smile. When I watch the sunrise as I drive to work, I see her smile. When I think of her throughout the day, I see her smile. When I see someone else smile, I see her smile. When I see a baby's face, I see her smile. When I drive home and see the sun set, I see her smile. When I read before I go to sleep, I see her smile. When I kiss her picture before I shut the light off, I see her smile. When I thank god I made it through another day without a drink, I see her smile.

This time alone gives me time to think. It's been a while since I've seen her smile. I used to wake up next to her in our bed. Now it's just a memory in my head. I used to do all those things, now she doesn't even own her rings. I gave all that up because I thought I knew. To have her back there isn't anything I wouldn't do. Now these memories are our past, that doesn't mean it has to last. I spend each day working on me, so maybe someday together we will be. The couple who was so very much in love, I pray each day to God above. I want to turn it around so what I saw is what I see. First I have to redefine me. With each day I continue to grow. I love her more each day from head to toe. It'll go back from I to we and from what I saw to what I see. When I wake up the first thing I see is her beautiful face smiling at me.

LETTING GO

By Hunter Dan

Sometimes the hardest part isn't letting go, it's convincing yourself what you already know. We argue about so many things, we argue until we take off our rings. You get mad at me, I get mad at you, what are we supposed to do. You don't hold back when you have something to say. I myself go the other way. There is so much I should get off my chest, but I hold it in thinking that's whats best.

I don't like to fight so I regress, when getting it out is probably whats best. I love you and you love me. Eye to eye we just don't see. I've made mistakes I will admit, sometimes I just don't give a shit. I'll make more because I am a guy, you will throw up your hands and ask me why. Are we to the point where we just give in, or band together and fight for the win. We have been through so much in five short years. You say they are long because they have been your tears. You love your man when he doesn't drink, it's a no brainer that he should stop and think.

I know it's a huge part of our deal, I justify it when I put you behind the wheel. Out for dinner you get to drive to preserve my license and keep it alive. I should see whats best and open my eyes, it could all work out if I stop the lies. So let go of the evil and grab onto what you feel is good, do whats right because you know you should. The hardest part isn't letting go, it's convincing yourself what you already know.

I URNED IT

By Hunter Dan

I saw the sunrise over the mountain, the days are numbered and I am counting. I take a swig and crack a beer. It doesn't matter the time, I have no fear. It's mid November and it's hunting season, I'm supposed to be hunting so that's the reason. I really don't need it, at the least I don't think I do, I'm heading into the woods so I'll only have a few. I'm parked at the spot and it's just a short walk. Luckily I'm alone, I may slur if I talk. I walk into the woods and sit down next to a tree and hope that a buck will meander by me. I close my eyes and fight falling asleep, a buck could sneak by and not make a peep. I could use the sleep my job keeps me up all night, between the booze and gravity I continue the fight. I try to balance this out in my mind, I may not be a good hunter but I'm one of a kind.

If I do fall asleep it would be a crime because the one you don't see will be the buck of a lifetime. Is that a deer? I see movement in the trees. There is something out there coming toward me. I pick up my rifle and spot it in the scope, yes it's a buck just as I had hoped. As he walks slowly I look at his horns, his head to the ground in search of acorns. He is coming straight at me and stops, he must have picked up my scent. As quick as he came, there he went. Are you kidding me, he must have smelled the gin and beer and said," what the hell is that smell? I'm outta here." I shake my head in disbelief, what the hell just happened to me?

I rewind the tape in my head and watch him come at me as he fed. To him this is life not just a sport, he turned and ran with one quick snort. I shake my head and walked back to my truck. A shot and a beer will change my luck. I tell myself this one more lie, but if I keep drinking like this I am going to die. My life just flashes before my eyes, I pound some more and start to cry. How many more will end my life, my next thought, what have I done to my wife? Tears stream down in my truck as I sit, whatever happens I URNED IT.

Inspirations and Emotions | 29

THE END

By Hunter Dan

It's not just a text but this message I send, it's a reminder to me you are still my friend. Without you around I can't stop thinking of you, and wondering what was I supposed to do. I didn't do this for me as I said I did, I this did for you, my emotions I hid. I didn't want you to choose me and to put me first. To come before your family made me feel worse. My respect for them was this decisions end, I had to let go of my best friend.

I don't want to live with hatred, I don't want to live with fear. I don't want my vision to be blurred by a tear. You have shown me courage and how to be strong. I need to keep these tools with me all life long. They don't like me for the things that I have done. My biggest regret is hurting their loved one. My heart hurts and continues to bleed, pumping blood to my muscles giving me the strength that need. I will remember the gentle kiss, and how my love felt inside you. That nothing could touch us, it was just me and you.

I don't regret the past nor wish to shut the door. My only regret is that I didn't do more. I don't think this is selfish, opening my hands to let you free. As you fly away I know you aren't coming back to me. It hurts for now, with every day that will end, I will be thankful I was saved by my best friend. I will be a better person I'm just not sure when, I know there is hope the sun will rise again. You know I will love you until the end of time, but when you hear those words it won't be the voice of mine.

So to you this poem is the last one I will write, I will walk away on a rope that hopefully is pulled tight. I made you laugh, I made you cry, I can only do one seeing you with another guy. I will keep my chin up as I wake up each day, and be thankful to you in what I say when I pray. As we stand heel to heel each looking the other way, we both take one step forward nothing more to say. I take a deep breath, and click the button to send, the last words are "I love you", THE END!

Land Of The Lockst

By Hunter Dan

This is a true poetic story of my journey recorded as I graciously received treatment at the Brattleboro Retreat. They have changed my life, and I am a better person for having had the honor and priveledge to experience sobriety through their program. I dedicate this story to my loving wife who endured years of alcoholic punishment. To my brother in law Kevin for teaching me the courage is in all of us, we just have to not be afraid to ask for help. And to the entire staff at Tyler 1, and to all at the Birches for teaching me how my life could again become manageable.

Lockst isn't really a word, it's a combination of where I was and the last sound that I heard. When I got here I was a mess, I would drink and hide it and it was time to confess. My wife and brother in law with compassion and love knew it was time I got help from above. February 23rd 2014 was the day that I arrived to get myself clean. I had tried and tried going to AA, it just wasn't working, what can I say. I thought I could do it I had done it before. But this time was different I couldn't open that door. It had a lock. I didn't have a key so I would just knock and knock. We walked through the door, the woman said have a seat, I am looking for the man my wife married at the Brattleboro Retreat.

I cry when I write, I cry when I read, I am begging for help I want to be freed. This is all I, it's not a we, because nobody ever tipped the bottle for me. It's not hell and it's not heaven, during my screening I blew a .17. I'm here for a while it's time to start, is getting here the hardest part? I hugged Kevin and I hugged Jen, not knowing when I'd ever see her again. It's called the Tyler House, if those walls could talk they've seen thousands of people go through detox. As we approached a door the man pulled out a key, he unlocked the door and said," follow me". As we walked down a hall he started to talk, he simply said, "welcome to the land of the lock". So now you know how the title came to be. It is time to start my new lifes journey.

He introduced me to a man who seemed kind of obscure, he showed me to my room and said," let me give you a tour". My room was on the short hall. One phone booth to share with no door at all. Two bathrooms down there that didn't seem bad, but if the place was full thats all the men had. Then we went down the long hall. One phone, one bath but no mens room at all. At the end of the hall was a room filled with couches, chairs and a large screen TV. He said," this is where all the meetings will be". We walked back toward my room as I looked at each face, a young girl actually welcomed me to this place. My laces wouldn't come out of my shoes, so I had to wear slippers, that was all I could do. The daily events were written on a board. Snacks and drinks were free but that was all I could afford. My wallet was home, I had a dollar on me, I don't really need it, so I'll just let it be.

They take your vital signs three times a day. They distribute the meds depending on what the results say. The nurses and counselors are all very nice. They do head checks every hour not once but at least twice. The meetings are frequent and they last about an hour. The TV goes out at 10:00, it's like they shut off the power. Lights out at 11:00, you have to go to bed. My wife's picture on my night stand, I kiss her on the head.

I woke up to voices in the hall. I looked at my watch because at 7:00 you can make a call. Some of the residents were up, they were the source of the noise. Dressed and ready to go no where like good girls and boys. It automatically arrived breakfast served at 8:00. Thank God there were sides there wasn't much on the plate. Same routine as yesterday the schedule on the board. You don't miss a meeting because everyone there, their name they record. Dr. Kane was my doctor, my social worker was Dan. They are both very nice and treated me like a man. I began to learn how all this would help. Not being dependant and figuring it out for myself. In an afternoon meeting we shared a favorite memory from our childhood. Two people spoke of their dog, they would have them back if they could. I shared Dog is God and revealed I had a hobby. The more that read it, the more wanted a copy. As the day went by more people started to care. So I brought out more poems and I began to share.

Even the staff enjoyed reading these. I was very honored when someone asked," can you autograph mine please". Here I am looking for help to stop drinking, my poems are helping others, thats what I'm thinking. They moved my room down to the other end of the hall. I still hear the voices, it's time to make a call. They needed my room for a man who threatened suicide. Someone sat at his door, he had nowhere to hide. My vitals are great, no more medication for me. The only thing left is take vitamin B. Dr. Kane and Dan agree it's time for the next phase. I completed detox in only three days.

After considering some options, and completing some searches, I agreed to try a program known as the Birches. I didn't miss a meeting I am proud to say. I'm even more proud they asked me to chair that nights meeting of AA. I said, "yes I can do it it's not a hard job, the format is simply layed out by Bill and Dr. Bob". The meeting went well, we even passed the basket, that dollar I had I put in the mini casket. The next day was Thursday, everyone wished me well. They care about their patients it's easy to tell. On the way out I got my shoes back. My clothes in a bag it was easy to pack. I went straight to the program, it started at 9:00. The man said," we would be late, but it would be fine". We dropped off my bag, I could pick it up at 3:00. Like the guy before he said, "follow me".

This is all new to me and seemed a little scary. We entered the small fish bowl and he introduced me to Carrie. She is my new social worker at the head of the table. I tried to remember all the names but I really wasn't able. Not knowing what to do or where anything was at, she asked if I could shadow this young man named Matt. When that group was over we had two more places to be, not only with Matt but with a charming young lady named Stephanie. When those were over I needed a lunch ticket, They took me to the reception area where I would be able to purchase it. I had my debit card numbers written on a receipt. The lady punched them in, but the machine couldn't complete. Rather than be late for lunch, Stephanie handed me two meal tickets. Not really knowing me she said, "later we'll get it fixed". Down a long tunnel to get something to eat. I have just gained two great friendships I would soon learn couldn't be beat. Meal tickets had a value of five dollars and that's it. I had more food on my plate, I thought I could take all that would fit. I went over by a dollar and change, Matt covered the differnce and I looked at him strange. These two just helped me when I couldn't help myself. Those good deeds are vested in my memory bank of wealth.

The afternoon classes start at 1:15. They recommended which one they thought was right for me. ACT is the one that I found myself in, if I follow the lead of Ellen this is a battle I can win. 2:15 to 3:00 is the last one of the day. Every day was different you choose from what ever the board would say. I gathered my stuff and headed over to the house that would be my new home. Along with my posessions I now had my cell phone. I was led to my room by Deb, she was nice as could be. I was now the newest resident of the house that's named Ripley. The room was very basic but I really didn't care. Jeff in the room next door, in between was a bathroom that we'd share. There is a kitchen that was shared by all, a TV room that followed suit. It was a place for conversation and to watch something on the tube.

The next day group started at 9:00. We shared what happened the day before and what was going on in our mind. Carrie asked questions about sleep and nutrition, to see if our goals simply came to fruition. As the days went by people would come and people would go. If it wasn't for this place these people I would never know. I have made so many friends from patients to staff. I have shed a few tears, but mostly I would laugh. Jenny and Peter run the 10:30 and 11:30 CD's. They are inspirational and informative to anyone like me. I brought my own breakfast, lunch and dinner, saving money every day. It was all made possible because we had the fridge and microwave. ACT at 1:15 and choosing whatever to end the day. Abby got my attention when she meditated my neck pain away.

At 3:00 all was said and done, completing two urine tests per week. If you do one on Monday then by Friday they will complete. Hanging in the evening, watching TV and talking to all. Going with them to meetings or just passing in the hall. Patrick who doesn't sleep that well, we would often stay up late. Watching anything on TV it was the conversations that were great. He's a man who has wisdom and his knowledge doesn't lack. I hope he got it right this time and never has to come back.

It's Friday March 14th and my time has drawn to an end. I want to leave the retreat not as a patient but a friend. Four days in Tyler, Twelve days in Ripley, believe it or not, the bed was hard to get used to, it was like sleeping on a cot. This poem is my story and many thanks to all at Anna Marsh Way, now I have a life to live and my disease is here to stay. I don't feel lost anymore, when I stood outside room 204, I didn't say a word. When I turned the key to lock the door, it was the last sound that I heard.

DAN

This year I turn 50 and I will be alcohol free. I'll be 58 and I too will be in recovery. My dog ran away and I recovered him. I think we make a good team. Together we can all defeat this. Alone we are nothing. Together we are everything. Yes you and your dog make a good team, for a purpose, and yes united we stand and divided we can fall. Despite my despondency the joy of fellowship is real though temporary. The thrill of life is often exemplory. I think we all need therapy. The power of a group is strong, attend 12 step meetings and you will be strong. Gain strength from those around you. And that is why we choose carefully. No matter what the outcome as a group we let the pen flow free.

CARLOS

It all started with the plane crash. Dazed I looked for a light. I felt solid ground below my body. My mind and soul were one. As I came out of my cacoon I found the light. Please stay within it, do not ever leave it again. But did the universe end as all light fades. How in the face of that do we remain hopeful. With the way this happened, it can be doubtful. Wow that was a mouthful. Hold on to the memory, it takes strenghth and courage to emerge out of the darkness into the light. The light is there as a guide, a source of brightness and warmth. To walk alone with no shoes, the ground so rough and to do it without a fight. There is always a light if we look for it. When I was swimming in the bottle.

BRANDON

I hope tomorrow is a brighter day. If the sun shines on me it will be. I anticipate spring like never before. Now that I have seen the sun I just want more. Spring is a happy time when everything grows. Mud beneath my feet and between my toes. I will take each day for the gift it is. Live for today, and the next will come. There is wisdom from each passing day. That is all we have, I have to say. Embrace life like a soothing salve. So it was and so it is. I will live each day as if it were Gods gift.

TIM

I wonder where the weekend has gone. Still sometimes the day is so long. When the days are so long and cold, I sit around and moan and groan. When time flies and things are moving I feel content. I'm participating in my own life so much more. It gives me hope. Here at the Birches I am learning the tools to cope. Being in therapy gives me hope. I am a stargazer lilly opening, claiming my space. It feels good to be here. Clearer in both mind and spirit. But sometimes the fog sets in. I find a way to let it be so I get through another day. Because a beautiful sunrise shall again show her face. another day full of hope and promise. Not always but often in good ways.

REBECCA

Seeking balance. Looking forward and up. Finding serenity. Seeking the whole. Big beautiful truth fall of treasures to behold and be a part of life that surrounds it. Have a romantic imagination. Trying to read this is aggravating. Still I sit here patiently waiting. To see if it comes out balanced and beautiful. Different poems in this world each unique and beautiful. With each passing to add a piece of ourselves. We all seek balance. I wandered lonely as a cloud.

JEFF

I am happy, for today I am not drinking. It is a blessing to be in the moment. It is in deed a blessing from God to have been given such a day to enjoy and be grateful for. You are an optimist. An overachiever we can't resist. I am grateful for today it is a gift. No matter how large or small, we must remember to stay in today. It is the ultimate gift. Tomorrow may bring challenges but I am more prepared for them. The more I read the more I like, I just want to read more. Every moment I have something to be grateful for. Praise those who help themselves. Let everything flow, never dwell or forget the past. Live for today for today is all we have.

JOHN

I enjoy the sun on my face. Being one with the sun. That is a beautiful observation to have and feel each day. And being aware of the time, I am just a small part of a poem, another line. No matter how small the part we play each is key. I am a small being, but I am not insignificant, I have importance. These lines I write for others are mere small parts of me. Each of us is a small cog in a large wheel, but all of us together make the whole. A smile is sunshine on your face. Acceptance as it comes is radiating grace. A single grain of sand can tip the balance to ones life. If you allow it to fall on the scale.

JOE

Lonliness is the memory of my childhood. With the dreams of thinking all is good. Wish I could say all is good. A child is a blessing and sees life as good. I can create new memories and the old ones might lose some of their power. That is when I realized that was the darkest hour. My lonliness is the memory of my wife and children, raising a family who are now grown and I am alone. There is joy in being on the right side of the grass. Soon it will be green again, I smell spring. The sunlight will help heal my soul. And the earth will keep me grounded.

Like my mood some days are gray and wintery, some are sunny and warm. Get ready to run the race of a life time. Can you teach me how?

HERB

My recovery is my main priority. Twas a brilliant thought it twas. Happiness just below the surface. Just waiting to bubble over the top. But then it stopped. As I reassessed my options, Drop back and lay low. Allow your heart to stay in and on a warm spirit. Spring is close. To lose yourself in spring, is pure joy. Try to stay in the moment and keep in line. Stay in the moment and everything will be fine. Put myself and recovery first, anything less can result in a mess. Focusing on myself and what I need is hard work. But to survive it all and rise above I feel I have been blessed. I havn't risen above all yet, but are learning the skills to have a chance.

WENDY

I am looking forward to sring. I can't wait to go outside and garden instead of feed the woodstove. While the hens are layin plenty. I am well grounded to the earth. But sometimes my head is in the clouds. May the fog lift, and become grounded in my spirit. Our heads in the clouds while our feet roam gods green earth. We go to the well of life and are happy to drink it. time to climb towards the light up out of the snakepit. Have confidence be firm, breath and not be cocky. Anticipate and embrace spring.

CPSIA information can be obtained at www.ICGtesting.com
Printed in the USA
BVOW05s2233170216
437129BV00001B/6/P